Recipes for the Soul

journal belongs to...

© 2016 Ranch House Press
All rights reserved. Printed in the United States of America.

www.annettebridges.com

ISBN: 978-1-946371-10-2

Journal Prompts

Recipes for the Soul

1. Recipes every soul food cook should know
2. Veggie soul food
3. Best southern soul macaroni & cheese
4. Soul food recipes that are almost as good as your mom's
5. Classic comfort food
6. Soul food recipes that will make you feel southern
7. Easy comfort food that always feeds your soul
8. Soul sweet taters
9. What music feeds your soul? Describe how it makes you feel.
10. Soul food make-over. Your own remake of a recipe you got from you mom, grandmother or mother-in-law or friend.
11. Soul cake recipes
12. Recipes your soul is asking for! Something new that looks enticing.
13. What is a book that inspires your soul again and again? Why?
14. Cooking like only mamma can! Your favorite recipes from your mom or grandmother.
15. Sugar & Soul. For the serious sweet tooth.
16. Soup recipes to warm your soul.
17. Glorious vacations that refuel your soul. Describe ones you've had or ones you dream about. What is it about them that is so reviving and refreshing?
18. Water recipes to cleanse your soul.
19. Soul bread recipes.
20. Crock pot soul food recipes.
21. Soul in wonder. Cooking with your favorite fruits.
22. Oven baked soul food.
23. Lyrics of the soul. What are the lyrics that speak to your soul in a way you'll never forget?
24. Soul seeker. Ask your friends to share their favorite soul food recipe.
25. Soul food rice dishes.
26. Chicken soup recipes to soothe the soul.
27. Yummy hot chocolate recipes to satisfy your soul.
28. Describe your most memorable meal times.
29. Fried chicken for the soul.
30. Romancing the soul. Candlelight dinner dishes and décor ideas.
31. Celebrating with soul. Holiday dishes to remember.

color your world

ABOUT the CREATOR

Annette Bridges is an author, publisher and women's retreat host on a mission to help every woman realize her story is extraordinary, valuable and noteworthy.

She has published the *Color Your World Journal Series* and formed a journal club to provide community, support and tools for women to record their ideas, feelings, experiences, memories and all the important details of their lives.

Before writing books and publishing journals and coloring books, this former public school and homeschool educator spent a decade writing hundreds of helpful, instructive, and light-hearted columns published by Texas newspapers, parenting magazines, websites and bloggers.

Annette lives on a Texas cattle ranch with her husband John, dachshund Lady and lots of cows. She can drive a tractor but only if wearing a fresh coat of lipstick and it's not her pedicure day!

You can learn more about Annette's books and products, blogs and videos as well as her women's retreats and other events at www.annettebridges.com.

Look for her on social media, too!

MESSAGE from the PUBLISHER

The **Color Your World Journal Series** is a pathway to self-discovery. It's where you write notes to yourself. Be your own cheerleader. Give yourself encouragement. Tell yourself what you're grateful for. Celebrate you!

There are countless reasons to keep a journal including collecting favorite recipes, listing goals and celebrating every experience and every one that's near and dear to you. A journal provides a home for the memories and lessons learned that you never want to forget.

Why a niche journal?

If you're anything like me, you have a journal (or even two or three journals) where you write anything and everything about anything and everything. My challenge comes when trying to find something I've written. I flip and flip through the pages of my two, three or four journals trying to find whatever it is. I never remember which journal I wrote down my whatever's!!

The solution? A niche journal! A journal that has a specific focus and theme! A journal where you can record your ideas, inspirations and things you want to remember in the appropriate journal.

Why big unlined paper?

Because big unlined paper is needed to record big ideas, dreams and memories! You need room to grow, stretch and expand. You need space to think beyond the confines of what you've always done, to pursue new dreams, discover your power and reimagine your purpose again and again. You need pages without lines and limitations to reconnect with your creative, perfectly imperfect self.

Plus, big unlined paper gives you space for more than words. You have plenty of room to doodle, draw or post photographs and clippings, too.

Why color is important?

When you journal, use colored pens and markers! Your world doesn't happen in black and white. Your life should be lived and written about in many colors. Even dark and sad memories feel lighter and brighter when told in color.

Journaling in color affects your mood and perception of your world. Colors evoke calm, cheer and comfort. Using color can lift your spirit and inspire your imagination. You may be surprised by all the beautiful benefits from adding more color into your life story.

When journaling, give yourself time to listen to your heart and reflect. Breathe in the moments. Feel. Be quiet. Let yourself be totally and thoroughly present with your thoughts. Let your heart transform you and teach you new insights. Open your mind to consider new ideas and possibilities. You may find that what your heart teaches will be life changing.

www.ingramcontent.com/pod-product-compliance
Lightning Source LLC
Chambersburg PA
CBHW051253110526
44588CB00025B/2978